"Toddler Treasure Hunt" is a work of fiction. This book is educational, interactive, and all images used were acquired using the Canva Pro subscription.

"Toddler Treasure Hunt" is Book One in the ongoing series, *Bright Beginnings for Little Learners*.

ISBN: 978-1-958023-59-4 Hardcover
ISBN: 978-1-958023-60-0 Paperback


Library of Congress Control Number: 2025927451

Written by Joan Enockson & Lynda Lowery
Graphic Designed by Joan Enockson

First printing, 2026
Laurens, IA

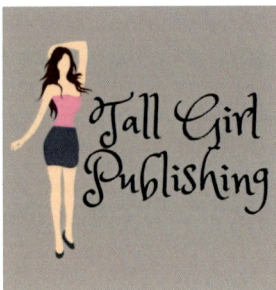

# Toddler Treasure Hunt

Joan Enockson
Lynda Lowery

**Bright Beginnings for Little Learners Series**

We are going on a
treasure hunt.

What will we find?

We found a purple purse.

# Can you find the purple flowers?

We are going on a treasure hunt.

What will we find?

We found a pink butterfly.

Can you find the
pink bow?

We are going on a treasure hunt.

What will we find?

We found a blue toothbrush.

Can you find the
blue blueberries?

We are going on a treasure hunt.

What will we find?

We found an orange orange.

# Can you find an orange basketball?

We are going on a
treasure hunt.

What will
we find?

We found green
leaves on a tree.

# Can you find the
# green grapes?

We are going on a
treasure hunt.

What will
we find?

We found a yellow car.

Can you find the
yellow banana?

We are going on a treasure hunt.

What will we find?

We found a red stop sign.

# Can you find

# the red scarf?

We are going on a
treasure hunt.

What will we find?

We found a black cat.

Can you find the
black hat?

We are going on a
treasure hunt.

What will we find?

We found a brown
table and chairs.

Can you find the
brown puppies?

We are going on a
treasure hunt.

What will we find?

We found a
white blanket.

Can you find the
white slippers?

# You did it!

# You found these treasures!

# Bright Beginnings for Little Learners

**Welcome to Bright Beginnings for Little Learners!** This playful preschool series is where curiosity leads the way! Each book invites toddlers and preschoolers on a joyful journey filled with discovery, from early letters and numbers to colors, shapes, and simple treasure hunts that spark problem-solving skills.

Along the way, little readers also learn important social-emotional lessons — like taking turns, helping friends, using kind words, and celebrating their own unique strengths.

Designed with bright visuals, easy prompts, and interactive seek-and-find moments, this series helps growing minds build confidence, learn new concepts, and explore their world with wonder. **It's the perfect first step into learning, laughter, and lifelong curiosity!**

**Ages 1-4**

# Meet the Co-Author

*Joan Enockson* blends her passion for education, music, and writing to create captivating children's books. With a deep understanding of children's social-emotional needs, she crafts stories that explore themes such as friendship, problem-solving, citizenship, and patriotism.

Having spent years teaching children of various ages in the public school system, Joan's experiences have shaped her writing style, allowing her to engage and intrigue young readers. She captivates their imaginations while incorporating life lessons that support 21st-century skills.

Joan takes young readers on thrilling adventures, encouraging them to explore their potential, develop critical thinking skills, and embrace values that promote personal growth and positive contributions to society. Her stories inspire children to embrace their individuality and empower them to become confident, compassionate, and active members of their communities.

*Joan Enockson's* dedication to education, music, and storytelling supports the creation of books that impact young minds. Her collaborative efforts with Lynda Lowery will enhance her efforts to shape the lives of countless children for generations to come.

# Meet the Co-Author

**Lynda Lowery** paused her career in the public sector when her oldest son was four years old. Her love for children motivated Lynda to create a daycare in her home. For decades, she has had the privilege of caring for hundreds of children, some of whom are now bringing their own children — a true testament to the bonds she has formed over the years!

The most rewarding experience for Lynda has been watching them grow into caring, responsible young adults. Memories of seeing their faces light up when they discover something new, or their excitement as they grasp new concepts, were key factors in challenging herself to write. Her stories are designed to help children learn by discovering their world.

Alongside caring for children, Lynda nurtures a passion for crafting. She expresses her creativity in various forms, including drawing, clay, painting, and more. Her love of crafting is shared by her sister, mother, and grandmother. Their hours of creating together were instrumental in helping Lynda develop concepts and activities empowering children to learn.

**Lynda** continues to be inspired by her daycare kids, who are always eager to help her create new ideas for her stories. Her collaboration with award-winning author and publisher Joan Enockson has helped Lynda take her stories to the next level.

# Tall Girl Publishing

## Ages 3-8

Counting Christmas Kittens

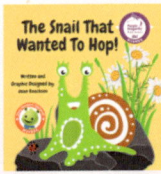
The Snail That Wanted To Hop!

El caracol que quería saltar!

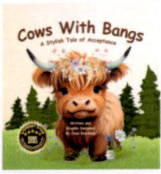
Cows With Bangs

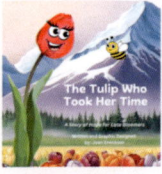
The Tulip Who Took Her Time

Moonbeam's Halloween Wish

Sleepy Kitty Sleeps

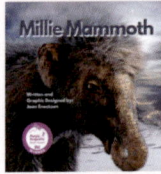
Millie Mammoth

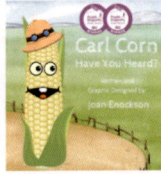
Carl Corn Have You Heard?

## Ages 8-12

FINDING GEORGE

CANDACE'S BIG AUDITION

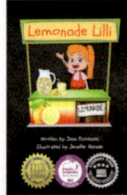
Lemonade Lilli

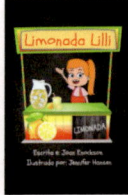
Limonada Lilli

STATE PARK

MEMORIAL DAY PARADE

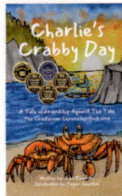
Charlie's Crabby Day

The Sand Sculpture Competition

Beneath the Blue

www.ingramcontent.com/pod-product-compliance
Lightning Source LLC
Chambersburg PA
CBRC091536260326
41914CB00019B/1633